The Making Of Bad Boys: Ride or Die

Revealing the Conception, History, Behind the Scenes and Storyline of the Movie

By

Kevin Cinemania

Copyrighted © 2024- Kevin Cinemania

All rights reserved

This work is protected by copyright law and cannot be reproduced, distributed, transmitted, published, displayed or broadcast without a prior written permission from the Author which is the copyright holder.

Unauthorized use duplication, dissemination of this work is strictly prohibited and may result in legal action.

Table Of Contents

Introduction

Chapter 1: Pre-Production Phase

Chapter 2: Production Insights

Chapter 3: Cast and Characters

Chapter 4: Filming and Action Sequences

Chapter 5: Music and Soundtrack

Chapter 6: Post-Production and Editing

Chapter 7: Marketing and Promotion

Conclusion

Introduction

The "Bad Boys" franchise is a series of action-comedy films that has been very successful since its inception, and it has managed to hold captive audiences worldwide. The franchise was brought to life by George Gallo, and it is famous for the wise-cracking detectives duo played by Will Smith and Martin Lawrence. It has changed over the years as it combined high-action episodes with humor endearing it more to those who love buddy cops movies.

The first installment of this movie came out in 1995 under the title "Bad Boys", which was directed by Michael Bay. It was through this film that people got introduced to Detectives Mike Lowrey (Will Smith) and Marcus Burnett (Martin Lawrence) who were two Miami narcotics officers with totally different characters. The main character, Mike, looked like a smooth talker while Marcus acted like a family man who had a more careful approach towards police work. They still however loved each other very much despite everything else that they had on their plates.

For instance, "Bad Boys," grossed above $141 million all over the world [et al] This fame can be associated with its combination of fast-paced action scenes; funny dialogue between protagonists; and a soundtrack that stays memorable for a long time afterwards. Thus, the movie created synergy between Will Smith and Martin Lawrence on screen while at same time serving as source material for subsequent additions to this franchise.

Another highly anticipated sequel, "Bad Boys II," was released in 2003 following the success of "Bad Boys." Michael Bay once again directed it and this time around he increased the stakes to a higher level with more explosive action sequences and some comedic moments. This is because there were a number of things that made it even more enjoyable to watch; including the hilarious interplay between Will Smith's character and his partner played by Martin Lawrence. Consequently, it became one of the biggest box office hits grossing over $273 million worldwide.

The Bad Boys franchise returned after many years in 2020 with a bang through "Bad Boys for Life." Directed by Adil & Bilall, this movie saw Will Smith and Martin Lawrence reprise their roles as two best friends who had to face new problems and adversaries. In addition to being hailed for its perfect mix of action, humor and sentimentality, Bad Boys for Life", was also a commercial success thereby accumulating an estimated sum of $426 million across the globe.

Fans were excited when it was announced that the fourth edition is "Bad Boys: Ride or Die." Another adrenaline pumping adventure featuring Detectives Mike Lowrey and Marcus Burnett awaits as main cast members from past films return alongside newcomers joining the ensemble.

Chapter 1: Pre-Production Phase

The process of creating a sequel to a successful film like "Bad Boys" is complex and intricate, needing a delicate balance of artistic vision, commercial considerations, and public expectations. The road from concept to production of "Bad Boys: Ride or Die," the fourth episode in the franchise, required strategic preparation, creative choices, and commitment from key partners.

The idea for a 'Bad Boys for Life' sequel began to take shape only shortly after its predecessor's success. Confirming that audiences still enjoyed these films and that there was more to be told about their characters and universe.

Sony Pictures, which controls the Bad Boys series, saw an opportunity to continue telling the story of Detectives Mike Lowrey (Will Smith) and Marcus Burnett (Martin Lawrence). At this point, Chris Bremner, who wrote the script for Bad Boys For Life, began developing a plot line for Part 4. Bremner was intimately familiar with their characters, particularly their relationships, so he devised a tale that would appeal to fans while introducing fresh elements to keep it intriguing.

Creating a sequel is unquestionably difficult because it requires finding the appropriate balance between paying homage to what came before and delivering something fresh. The directors Adil and Bilall, as well as other creative team members, were responsible for modifying the characters while keeping their characteristics intact. This featured Mike and Marcus' personal growth, changing dynamics in their friendship, and a variety of problems that they had to overcome.

Furthermore, the casting decisions made had significant ramifications for "Bad Boys: Ride or Die." It was critical to keep some prominent players, such as Will Smith and Martin Lawrence, in order to preserve continuity and draw viewers, while also featuring new faces in the tale. Vanessa Hudgens, Alexander Ludwig, and Paola Núñez were among the cast members who contributed to the plot in various ways.

The concept for "Bad Boys: Ride or Die" was written to provide a compelling story that would appeal to both long-time fans of the franchise and newcomers. The script was reworked multiple times to ensure that it included enough action scenes, comedic moments, and emotional highlights to function well. The film explores issues such as friendship and loyalty, among others, which complicates the characters' motivations.

Moving on, there were hurdles to overcome, such as scheduling conflicts, logistical issues, and artistic decisions. The performers' and technicians' joint efforts, combined with studio and production team assistance, contributed to the development of Bad Boys: Ride or Die.

Making a movie is a precise art form that involves creative vision, strategic planning, and collaborative effort. Starting over from the beginning to get it ready for production was focussed on providing a sequel that will entertain, excite, and stick with fans, thereby extending the Bad Boy series history.

Script Writer

When it comes to creating the narrative for Bad Boys 4, Bremner provides a new viewpoint and originality. As an action-comedy screenwriter who had previously worked on numerous films, he was expected to come up with an intriguing tale that would be used to expand on the previous Bad Boys films while also including some fresh elements that would keep audiences interested.

Bremner had to understand the franchise's core elements when writing the script for "Bad Boys: Ride or Die," such as the dynamic between Detectives Mike Lowrey (Will Smith) and Marcus Burnett (Martin Lawrence), high-risk action sequences, and the humor mixed with emotions that are at the heart of these films. The idea was to construct a plot that will appeal to old fans while also attracting new youthful viewers.

Extensive research and brainstorming meetings marked the start of the screenwriting process. He carefully examined character development, themes, arcs, and audience feedback on prior "Bad Boys" films. This first stage helped him realize crucial ideas and episodes that would serve as the foundation for "Bad Boys: Ride or Die."

Bremner has an advantage over others in his trade because he can combine intense action with character-driven storytelling. Thus, in "Bad Boys: Ride or Die," he delved deeper into Mike and Marcus' personalities by exploring their pasts, motivations for their actions, and psychological growth. The addition added tremendous depth to their acting, raising it above simply adrenaline-fueled occurrences.

Collaboration was crucial in the scriptwriting process. Working with the directorial team, which included Adil and Bilall, he ensured that the screenplay fit within their concept for the film. This included regular meetings, feedback sessions, and modifications to improve both the story and the language.

Finding the perfect balance between keeping memories from previous films and introducing new elements was one of the challenges Bremner encountered. He wanted "Bad Boys: Ride or Die" to seem like an organic continuation of the franchise while still moving it to new areas. This meant developing interesting new characters, weaving intriguing plot twists, and delving into themes like atonement, family, and resilience.

The writing process also required painstaking attention to detail when it came to action situations. Bremner worked with those in charge of stunts and special effects to ensure that all action scenes were exhilarating while also contributing to character arcs and the overall flow of the narration. Bremner's scriptwriting abilities, in particular, aided in maintaining the balance inherent in the 'Bad Boys' franchise.

The script for "Bad Boys: Ride or Die" had numerous versions and adjustments as it progressed. The cast, director, and studio executives provided feedback to help improve the dialogue, pacing, and character development. The final screenplay established a balance between the spirit of 'Bad Boy' while pushing boundaries and providing a vivid, contemporary cinematic experience.

Casting decisions and returning cast members

The casting decisions for "Bad Boys: Ride or Die" were critical to the production of the fourth installment in the series. This constellation, which included both veterans and newcomers, was carefully chosen to produce a dynamic and fascinating collection of characters that would appeal to viewers.

Among the most anticipated aspects of "Bad Boys: Ride or Die" was the return of key cast members who had become inseparable from the franchise. Will Smith returned as Detective Lieutenant Michael Eugene "Mike" Lowrey, resuming his typical charm and wit on screen. Martin Lawrence also returned as Detective Lieutenant Marcus Miles Burnett, showcasing his comedic timing and connection with Smith.

As a result, their comeback not only paid homage to the franchise's past, but also took advantage of their fame and massive fan base that had grown over time. As such, Mike and Marcus are icons; they were on screen partners whose participation catapulted prior "Bad Boys" films to popularity, so their return represented continuity and familiar faces for moviegoers.

Smith and Lawrence were joined by numerous cast members who reprised their roles from "Bad Boys for Life" (2020). Vanessa Hudgens returned as Kelly, the weapons expert for AMMO (Advanced Miami Metro Operations). Alexander Ludwig reprised his role as Dorn, AMMO's technical guru. Paola Núñez reprised her role as Captain Rita Secada, the commander of the Miami Police unit AMMO and Mike's former lover. These are characters who returned to the plot to show how much they had evolved since the film.

Along with the recurring casts, a few brilliant actors appeared in "Bad Boys: Ride or Die." Eric Dane joined the cast as the villain Banker, providing Mike and Marcus with a formidable opponent. Ioan Gruffudd also joined the franchise, playing a character that has yet to be revealed. Melanie Liburd demonstrated her acting abilities as seen in television shows such as 'This Is Us'. Tiffany Haddish, known for her comedic performances, is also in the cast, indicating that this picture will be filled with fun and energy.

"Bad Boys: Ride or Die" evaluated numerous aspects in casting, including the characters' relevance to the plot, as well as the availability and suitability of the actors, in addition to the desire for new voices in the picture. The ensemble cast included both familiar stars and newcomers, promising a dynamic and enjoyable cinematic experience that will captivate audiences while paying tribute to the Bad Boys franchise's past.

Overall, casting for "Bad Boys: Ride or Die" demonstrated a delicate mix of continuity and change, ensuring that the fourth edition resonated with both fans and newcomers. With brilliant actors playing these roles, another exciting adventure with Detectives Marcus Burnett and Mike Lowrey had begun.

22

Chapter 2: Production Insights

Behind-the-scenes Filming Location

Filming locations play an important role in shaping a film's visual identity and atmosphere, and "Bad Boys: Ride or Die" is no exception. A sneak peek into filming locations provides insight into the creative decisions made by the production personnel, as well as how these surroundings affect the overall theatrical experience.

Miami's beautiful beauty was instrumental in capturing "Bad Boys: Ride or Die" on film. Miami, with its golden beaches, multicolored art deco houses, and vibrant city centers, provided an exhilarating backdrop for action-packed movie sequences and scenes where people met their fate.

To strengthen the storyline and bring the universe of "Bad Boys: Ride or Die" to life, the production crew scouted locations throughout Miami. Every site, from Ocean Drive to South Beach, as well as some lesser-known districts and metropolitan areas, was meticulously chosen to provide viewers with a genuine sense of authenticity in each scene.

The famous Art Deco section in Miami Beach was one of the most visible filming locations for 'Bad Boys: Ride or Die'. The area's brilliant colors, distinctive architectural elements, and lively atmosphere made it an ideal location for some key sequences in the film. The film contrasts Mike Lowrey's slick modern style with the edgy aspect of metropolitan areas, which visually enhances the plot.

Aside from Miami Beach, the production crew employed other portions of Miami and its surrounding areas to create distinct locations for various sequences. From luxurious waterfront houses to gritty downtown streets, each location added depth and ambiance to the picture, improving the overall cinematic experience.

Furthermore, "Bad Boys: Ride or Die" expanded beyond Miami to include other locations that played key parts in the plot. Including dynamic action scenes situated in locations such as industrial warehouses, busy city streets, and attractive coastal areas provided variety and excitement to the color palette employed in film production.

This behind-the-scenes look at on-location shooting demonstrates how these sets are brought to life, as well as the creative choices and logistics involved. Liaisons with local officials and permission acquisition are the first steps, followed by the creation of intricate action scenes.

The utilization of genuine locations and real-world surroundings adds authenticity and depth to "Bad Boys: Ride or Die," completely immersing viewers in the film's world and improving the overall cinematic experience. Behind-the-scenes attempts to recreate the essence of Miami and other key places highlighted the production process's meticulous attention to detail and commitment to quality.

This behind-the-scenes look at the filming locations for "Bad Boys: Ride or Die" underlines the importance of the place in crafting a film's aesthetic. From well-known Miami landmarks to gritty urban slums, each location contributed significantly to the Bad Boys franchise world and gave spectators an exhilarating immersive cinematic experience.

Challenges and highlights during principal photography

Principal photography for a film like "Bad Boys: Ride or Die" entails numerous challenges and highlights that influence the production process and contribute to the overall quality of the finished product. From dramatic action sequences to capturing emotive performances, the filming process is fraught with both victory and complexity.

One of the most difficult tasks during primary photography was orchestrating the spectacular action sequences that have become synonymous with "Bad Boys" films. This meant that the production staff was responsible for ensuring the safety of the cast and crew while simultaneously giving viewers with adrenaline-pumping moments like as car chases, gunfights, and explosions. This requires extensive planning, collaboration with stunt teams, and rigorous adherence to safety requirements.

Given that Miami was shot on location in unpredictable locations such as open streets, coordinating action sequences proved difficult. All aspects of production, from navigating congested streets to determining how directors can communicate with local officials granting permits and monitoring traffic, had to be meticulously managed for the flawless execution of striking action scenes.

In addition to action scenes, the main focus of the photography was on capturing the franchise's emotional depths and human interactions. Will Smith and Martin Lawrence, as well as other members of the ensemble, delivered performances that helped to convey the humor, drama, and friendship that underpin the film. To capture genuine and fascinating performances, we used a combination of screenplay direction, on-the-spot actor improvisation, and directorial assistance.

Managing logistics during principal photography was another problem. The production crew worked long hours liaising with local crews and suppliers, as well as obtaining equipment and lodgings for numerous locations, to ensure a seamless workflow and efficient resource usage. This necessitated long working hours, strict scheduling, and adaptability to unexpected obstacles that frequently arise during filming.

Despite this, there were several highlights during main photography for "Bad Boys: Ride or Die". Adil and Bilall (directorial duo), Robrecht Heyvaert (cinematographer), and a skilled cast/crew collaborated to produce breathtaking visual sequences, dramatic camera movements, and unforgettable performances that brought a story to life.

One of the pleasures of main photography was the cast's camaraderie both on and off set, as well as the team's synergy. The connection between Will Smith and Martin Lawrence, as well as the inclusion of new characters such as Vanessa Hudgens, Eric Dane, and Tiffany Haddish, improved the series' acting dynamics and made them more authentic and meaningful.

Throughout primary photography, the cast and crew maintained a high level of professionalism and devotion to excellence. The approach involved a lot of teamwork and creative direction, where strong action sequences were coupled with real emotions expressed by actors to offer a flawless picture of what the "Bad Boys" brand is all about.

This article has demonstrated that making a movie is not a simple endeavor because there are numerous hurdles encountered during principal filming, such as those listed in this paper, but it was through these difficulties that good results were achieved, finally leading to success. The approach entailed coordinating actions taking place in several geographical areas to create an action-packed video that captured fantastic performances from all of the actors involved, all of whom faced logistical challenges, necessitating devotion, teamwork, and innovative problem solution. While honoring their past through intriguing narratives, this resulted in a spectacular visual experience for audiences, pushing them beyond their expectations and enthralling them.

Role of directors Adil & Bilall in shaping the film

Adil El Arbi and Bilall Fallah, often known as Adil & Bilall, were the directors of the film "Bad Boys: Ride or Die". The fourth installment of the "Bad Boys" series turned out this way thanks to their creative vision, directorial expertise, and collaborative tactics.

Adil and Bilall brought to "Bad Boys: Ride or Die" the capacity to integrate action-packed moments with character-driven tales, among other things. They knew how to achieve a balance between adrenaline-pumping excitement and emotional intricacy in individual individuals' narratives. In doing so, they created an account that viewers could relate to on a variety of levels, ranging from adrenaline-pumping actions to comedic relief moments.

While maintaining true to the franchise's key features, the filmmaking duo offered some fresh ideas. Even though they displayed parts of their own general thinking and cinematic tastes, they were not hesitant to employ distinctive styles like as dynamic camera work, fast-moving visuals, and extremely energetic sequences, as seen in Bad Boys films.

They took a collaborative approach to the art and craft of filmmaking, working closely with the cast and crew to bring their vision to life. They created a supportive and creative environment on set, encouraging performers to develop their personalities and bring realism to their performances. This collaboration was crucial in developing chemistry among cast members, which improved the film's overall dynamics.

Their work with the cinematographer, production designer, and other key creatives intended to produce a consistent and visually appealing film. Their work demonstrated meticulousness, visual narrative skills, and intricacy in execution, as seen by what was seen after completion, resulting in a thrilling cinematic experience.

Given the director's background with action films, this became immediately apparent when shooting action sequences for this picture. Adil and Bilall injected dynamic energy into these scenes, resulting in fearfully obstreperous car chases and violent gunfights, yet it had always appeared to be a natural progression.

Beyond the action, Adil and Bilall concentrated on the film's emotional heart, delving into the characters' psychological journeys and exploring themes of redemption, devotion, and family. This brought depth and relevance to the story, transforming "Bad Boys: Ride or Die" from a collection of action-packed scenes to a captivating and engaging narrative.

Chapter 3: Cast and Characters

In "Bad Boys: Ride or Die," a strong ensemble cast plays significant roles, each adding depth, charisma, and complexity to their characters. Let's get into a character analysis of some of the film's important roles:

1. Detective Lieutenant Michael Eugene "Mike" Lowrey [Will Smith]

Mike Lowrey is the charismatic and suave investigator that makes up one half of the renowned "Bad Boys" pair. Will Smith's portrayal of Mike combines confidence, wit, and vulnerability. Mike is noted for his fast mind, keen abilities, and unrelenting commitment to justice. However, beneath his rough appearance lurks a strong sense of loyalty and morality, particularly toward his colleague, Marcus Burnett. Throughout the film, Mike struggles with personal issues and confronts his history, bringing complexity to his character journey.

2. Detective Lieutenant Marcus Miles Burnett (Martin Lawrence)

Marcus Burnett is Mike Lowrey's family-oriented, cautious antithesis. Marcus is portrayed by Martin Lawrence in a way that is both funny and heartfelt. Marcus is noted for his humorous timing, down-to-earth nature, and undying dedication to his partner, Mike. Despite his early hesitation to participate in perilous circumstances, Marcus proves to be an invaluable asset to the duo's exploits, demonstrating courage and tenacity when the stakes are high. Throughout the film, Marcus struggles to balance his personal life with his responsibilities as a detective, resulting in moments of reflection and growth.

3. Kelly (Vanessa Hudgens)

Kelly is AMMO's competent weapons expert and a fresh addition to the "Bad Boys" universe. Vanessa Hudgens' portrayal of Kelly exudes toughness, intelligence, and resourcefulness. Kelly is noted for her strategic thinking, technical expertise, and relentless commitment to her team. Kelly, a critical member of AMMO, navigates high-pressure circumstances with confidence and precision, demonstrating her combat and teamwork ability. Kelly's interactions with the rest of the team, particularly Mike and Marcus, provide dimension to her character growth throughout the film.

4. Captain Rita Secada (Paola Núñez)

Captain Rita Secada is Mike's ex-girlfriend and the commander of the Miami Police Department's AMMO section. She brings a mix of power, knowledge, and emotional complexity to the character. Paola Núñez's portrayal of Rita embodies professionalism, leadership, and personal history. Rita is noted for her strong personality, smart thinking, and commitment to upholding the law. Rita, a crucial player in the film, faces the trials of leading her team while also dealing with past relationships and personal issues. Her interactions with Mike, Marcus, and the other characters give layers of drama and emotion to the story.

5. The Banker (Eric Dane)

Banker is the principal enemy in "Bad Boys: Ride or Die," and he plays the part with terror, cunning, and cruelty. Eric Dane's portrayal of Banker exudes controlled ferocity and presence. Banker is renowned for his criminal mastermind methods, strategic planning, and ability to keep one step ahead of law enforcement. Banker's clashes with Mike, Marcus, and the rest of the team propel the story forward, resulting in high-stakes action and spectacular showdowns.

Chapter 4: Filming and Action Sequences

Stunt coordination and action choreography are essential components of a film like "Bad Boys: Ride or Die," which relies heavily on high-octane action sequences to drive the narrative and engage moviegoers. The behind-the-scenes effort required to create these spectacular moments is painstaking preparation, precise coordination, and a determined team of professionals.

The stunt coordination for "Bad Boys: Ride or Die" was overseen by seasoned specialists who specialize in creating and carrying out intricate action sequences that are both visually stunning and safe for the cast and crew. This was a multi-step process that started with designing the action beats and choreographing the movements to enhance impact and realism.

One of the most important components of stunt coordination was to ensure the performers' safety during intense action situations. This required extensive training, rehearsals, and the use of specialized equipment to reduce hazards and ensure that each feat was completed with accuracy and control. Car chases, hand-to-hand combat, and gunfights were all methodically planned and executed to provide maximum excitement while prioritizing safety.

The action choreography for "Bad Boys: Ride or Die" was another important factor in bringing the film's thrilling moments to life. Skilled stunt performers and combat choreographers collaborated closely with the cast to plan and rehearse the precise actions and sequences that would appear on screen. This entailed combining martial arts, tactical moves, and dynamic camera work to produce smooth and dramatic action scenes.

The cooperation of stunt performers, actors, and the camera team was critical to portraying the intensity and authenticity of the action sequences. This necessitated exact timing, clear communication, and a thorough comprehension of the choreography to guarantee that every punch, kick, and stunt landed successfully on film. The end effect was a seamless blend of action and storyline that kept fans interested and engrossed in the film's high-stakes setting.

The automobile chase scene in "Bad Boys: Ride or Die" was one of the most memorable action sequences, requiring careful coordination between stunt drivers, practical effects companies, and the directing crew. From traversing tiny streets to performing precise movements, the car chase scene demonstrated the stunt coordination team's competence and talent in providing heart-pounding thrills while adhering to safety requirements.

In addition to standard action sequences, the film had dramatic gunfights and hand-to-hand combat scenes that necessitated painstaking preparation and training. Coordination between actors and stunt performers was critical in bringing these moments to life, ensuring that each movement and interaction appeared authentic and dramatic on film.

Overall, the stunt coordination and action choreography in "Bad Boys: Ride or Die" contributed to the film's unique blend of thrill, intensity, and spectacle. The stunt crews' passion and ability, together with the collaboration of actors and crew, produced spectacular action moments that brought depth and excitement to the entire cinematic experience.

Technical aspects of recording high-intensity situations

High-octane scenes, such as violent action sequences, automobile chases, and explosive moments, require a variety of technical factors to capture the intensity and realism required. In "Bad Boys: Ride or Die," the technical crew faced unique hurdles and relied on specific technology and techniques to bring these moments to life.

One of the most important technical components of filming high-speed scenes is the usage of specialized camera rigs and equipment. For action-packed scenes such as automobile chases, the production team used a variety of camera mounts, including car-mounted rigs, drones, and handheld cameras, to achieve dynamic and immersive pictures from diverse angles. This enabled for smooth movement and close-up shots that immersed viewers in the action, boosting the overall cinematic experience.

The utilization of stunt doubles and actors added to the realism of high-octane situations. Skilled stunt performers were used to do daring maneuvers, jumps, and feats that would be too dangerous for the main ensemble. This required rigorous planning, safety standards, and preparation to guarantee that each stunt was performed safely and convincingly on camera.

In addition to camera setups and stunt performers, special and practical effects were essential for filming high-octane scenes. Explosions, crashes, and other dramatic moments were created using a combination of real effects (pyrotechnics and physical props) and visual effects (CGI improvements). The combination of realistic and computer effects provided depth and realism to the action sequences, resulting in visually breathtaking moments that increased the film's thrill.

Sound design and engineering are another technical part of recording fast-paced situations. Sound is essential in increasing the impact and intensity of action sequences, from the boom of engines during a car chase to the shooting and explosions in a violent encounter. Sound experts used specialized microphones, equipment, and procedures to produce clean and powerful sounds that complimented the visual extravaganza on screen, immersing spectators in the adrenaline-fueled action.

Coordination among the technical team, which included camera operators, stunt coordinators, special effects artists, and sound engineers, was critical to performing high-octane scenes smoothly. Clear communication, rigorous preparation, and rehearsal were critical in ensuring that all technical aspects worked together to create thrilling and dramatic moments that resonated with spectators.

Furthermore, post-production editing and visual effects greatly improved the technical aspects of high-octane situations. From improving physical effects to adding digital refinements, the post-production crew labored to achieve a unified and impactful final product.

Overall, the technical aspects of recording high-speed scenes in "Bad Boys: Ride or Die" necessitated a combination of specialized technology, competent specialists, meticulous planning, and perfect collaboration. The technical team used novel techniques and technology to convey the excitement, intensity, and realism that define these thrilling moments on screen, contributing to the film's overall success and immersion.

Chapter 5: Music and Soundtrack

Lorne Balfe's music for the film "Bad Boys: Ride or Die" adds depth, drama, and intensity to important moments in the film. Balfe's talent in creating scores for action films was evident in his work on "Bad Boys: Ride or Die," where his music matched the high-octane moments and enhanced audiences' entire cinematic experience.

Lorne Balfe's ability to capture the energy and excitement of the action sequences was one of his most valuable contributions to the film. Balfe's music, with its dynamic and rhythmic compositions, complemented the film's fast-paced automobile chases, furious gunfights, and thrilling scenes. The use of driving rhythms, throbbing beats, and orchestral compositions created a sense of urgency and adrenaline to these situations, increasing their impact and immersing spectators in the heart-pounding action.

Balfe's score also contributed significantly to the film's emotional depth. Beyond the action, "Bad Boys: Ride or Die" delves into themes of devotion, repentance, and personal growth, which Balfe's music reflects through heartbreaking melodies, passionate strings, and evocative motifs. His ability to elicit a wide spectrum of emotions through music brought depth to the characters and tale, resulting in a more immersive and compelling narrative experience.

In addition to boosting action and emotion, Balfe's music helped to create the film's overall atmosphere and tone. The usage of thematic motifs, repeating musical components, and various instrumentation contributed to "Bad Boys: Ride or Die"'s distinct musical character. Whether depicting the bustling streets of Miami, the tension of a dramatic scene, or the camaraderie between people, Balfe's compositions enriched the visual storytelling and brought the film's environment to life.

Balfe's collaborative attitude with the filmmaking crew and sound engineers was another important part of his contribution to the film. Balfe worked closely with the producers to ensure that his music flowed smoothly with the film's visuals, tempo, and narrative beats. This partnership resulted in a unified and immersive audio-visual experience that resonated with audiences and enhanced the overall cinematic impact of "Bad Boys: Ride or Die."

Furthermore, Balfe's soundtrack for the picture demonstrated his ability to merge classic orchestral components with electronic instrumentation and current soundscapes. This hybrid approach to writing music gave the soundtrack a modern edge and cinematic flair, making it both accessible to viewers and relevant to the film's genre and style.

Overall, composer Lorne Balfe's contribution to "Bad Boys: Ride or Die" helped shape the film's auditory landscape and increase its storytelling effect. Through dynamic compositions, expressive themes, and a collaborative approach with the filmmaking team, Balfe's music highlighted important moments, heightened emotions, and gave a memorable musical dimension to spectators' entire cinematic experience.

Sound design and soundtrack selection procedure

The sound design and soundtrack selection process for a film like "Bad Boys: Ride or Die" is rigorous, resulting in an immersive audio experience that compliments the visuals and enriches the plot. Sound design and soundtrack choices play an important role in crafting the overall cinematic experience, from capturing the sounds of high-octane action moments to choosing music that connects with the film's tone and themes.

The sound design for "Bad Boys: Ride or Die" began with recording and generating audio elements to improve the realism and impact of the film's action sequences. This entailed capturing realistic sounds of motors revving, tires squealing, shooting, explosions, and other environmental sounds that would be used in the film's audio mix. The idea was to create a sense of immersion and realism, giving viewers the impression that they were right in the heart of the action.

In addition to recording genuine noises, the sound design team used techniques including foley artistry and sound effects editing to improve and layer audio aspects. Foley artists added depth and realism to the audio mix by recreating small noises like footfall, clothing rustling, and item interactions. Sound effects editors then meticulously chose and modified a library of sounds to create memorable moments and improve the dynamics of the action sequences.

The soundtrack selection process for "Bad Boys: Ride or Die" included selecting songs that would match the film's tone, themes, and story beats. This involved picking instrumental music, creative compositions, and licensed songs to heighten the emotional depth, intensity, and mood of important situations. The soundtrack selection process was a joint effort between the director, composer, music supervisor, and sound designers to ensure that the music matched the film's vision.

One of the most important aspects of soundtrack selection was selecting music that resonated with the characters and plot arcs of "Bad Boys: Ride or Die." This entailed choosing tunes that matched the personality of characters such as Mike Lowrey and Marcus Burnett, as well as conveying the intensity and thrill of action-packed scenes. The soundtrack included a variety of genres such as hip-hop, electronic, symphonic, and rock, resulting in a complex and dynamic musical landscape that complemented the visuals.

The collaboration of the sound design team, composer Lorne Balfe, and music supervisors was critical in creating a soundtrack that improved the overall cinematic experience. Balfe's original score merged smoothly with selected songs and sound effects, resulting in a unified aural narrative that heightened emotions, increased tension, and emphasized crucial points in the film.

Furthermore, the sound design and music selection processes required thorough editing, mixing, and mastering to guarantee a balanced and impactful audio mix. Sound engineers used cutting-edge equipment and software to fine-tune each sound element, modify levels, and create spatial effects that improved the immersive quality of the audio experience.

The sound design and soundtrack selection process for "Bad Boys: Ride or Die" was collaborative and careful, with the goal of providing consumers with an immersive aural experience. From collecting genuine noises to producing a broad and dynamic soundtrack, the sound design team and music collaborators were important in molding the overall cinematic impact and improving the film's storytelling.

Chapter 6: Post-Production and Editing

The editing and finalization of the film are critical steps in bringing all aspects together to create a cohesive and engaging cinematic experience. In the case of "Bad Boys: Ride or Die," the editing process entailed honing the storytelling, improving visual and audio aspects, and maintaining a smooth flow from beginning to end.

The editing process for "Bad Boys: Ride or Die" started with compiling the raw footage shot during principal photography. This entailed analyzing and sorting the material, picking the finest takes, and putting them in a rough order based on the narrative and storyboard. The editor worked closely with the director and other important stakeholders to determine the film's pacing, tone, and overall structure.

One of the most important components of the editing process was creating action sequences that were exciting and impactful. This included removing extraneous scenes, improving visual effects and sound design, and maintaining a fast-paced rhythm to keep spectators interested. The idea was to produce fluid and energetic action sequences that flowed seamlessly within the film's narrative structure.

In addition to action sequences, the editing process emphasized character development, emotional beats, and thematic continuity. Scenes displaying character interactions, moments of levity, and dramatic tension were meticulously edited to ensure they resonated with audiences and contributed to the broader story arc. Transitions between scenes, visual effects enhancements, and auditory cues were all fine-tuned during the editing process to produce a finished and consistent film.

The editing crew worked closely with the sound design and music departments to smoothly include audio elements into the final cut. This entailed fine-tuning sound effects, altering volumes, and syncing music cues to increase emotional impact and immerse viewers in the film's universe. Balancing dialogue, music, and sound effects to produce a dynamic audio mix was an important part of completing the film's audiovisual presentation.

Visual effects and CGI upgrades were also important parts of the editing process for "Bad Boys: Ride or Die." The post-production crew used digital effects, green screen composites, and CGI elements to improve action scenes, create realistic landscapes, and bring the film's visual splendor to life. The editor collaborated closely with visual effects artists to guarantee a smooth integration and professional visual appearance.

Color grading and correction were critical in creating the film's atmosphere, tone, and visual appeal. The colorist worked to improve contrasts, alter lighting, and provide a uniform color palette that matched the director's concept and the general style of the "Bad Boys" franchise. This final addition provided depth and visual richness to the film's cinematography, improving the overall viewing experience.

After the editing process was completed, the finishing stage entailed assessing the film, making any necessary tweaks or revisions, and preparing the final deliverables for distribution. This entailed making digital copies, mastering audio tracks, and ensuring that technical requirements met industry standards for theatrical distribution, streaming platforms, and home media.

Editing and finishing the film for "Bad Boys: Ride or Die " required a complete approach to shaping the visual and audio aspects, enhancing storytelling, and producing a coherent cinematic experience. The editing team contributed significantly to the film's polished and impactful final form by working together, paying attention to detail, and having technical expertise.

Visual effects and CGI improvements

Visual effects (VFX) and computer-generated imagery (CGI) enhancements play an important role in modern filmmaking, particularly in action movies like "Bad Boys: Ride or Die." These approaches enable filmmakers to create magnificent and immersive sequences that challenge the conventions of visual storytelling. In "Bad Boys: Ride or Die," VFX and CGI additions gave depth, authenticity, and spectacle to crucial scenes throughout the film.

One of the key uses of visual effects and CGI in "Bad Boys: Ride or Die" was to create realistic and exciting action sequences. Scenes including automobile chases, explosions, and fierce combat benefited from visual effects advancements that increased audience enthusiasm and intensity. CGI, for example, was utilized to augment practical effects like creating realistic explosions, debris, and damage during action scenes, whereas VFX enabled the seamless integration of digital elements into live-action film.

CGI was used to design and animate digital characters and animals that interacted with the live-action cast. This includes building digital counterparts for stunt performers, animating vehicles and objects, and improving ambient components to produce immersive and visually appealing scenes on screen. These CGI additions provided realism and spectacle to the film's action scenes, making them more dynamic and exciting for viewers.

Visual effects were also used to create expansive and intricate locations, broadening the scope of the film. CGI was employed to construct huge cityscapes, intricate set pieces, and immersive backgrounds, all of which contributed to the film's world-building and visual storytelling. This allows them greater creative freedom in depicting locales, scenarios, and situations that would be difficult or prohibitive to film using only practical methods.

In addition to action sequences and locations, visual effects and CGI were used to create futuristic and high-tech components that are crucial to the film's story. This includes creating and animating future cars, gadgets, and digital interfaces to bring a sense of innovation and technology to the universe of "Bad Boys: Ride or Die." These CGI additions served to define the film's futuristic environment and added to the overall look and style of narrative.

Collaboration among visual effects artists, CGI animators, and the filmmaking team was critical in implementing these advancements successfully. The VFX team was able to map out and execute complicated visual sequences that flawlessly merged with the live-action material thanks to meticulous preparation, concept art, storyboarding, and pre-visualization. To achieve the intended visual impact, we used cutting-edge technologies, digital rendering techniques, and artistic ingenuity.

Furthermore, the usage of visual effects and CGI in "Bad Boys: Ride or Die" went beyond action moments, incorporating subtle additions and corrections that improved the film's overall visual quality. This comprised digital compositing, color grading, matte painting, and image modification techniques to improve the cinematography, lighting, and visual aesthetics of each shot.

Visual effects and CGI advancements significantly improved the visual storytelling, realism, and spectacle of "Bad Boys: Ride or Die." These approaches, which included explosive action sequences, immersive locations, and futuristic aspects, added to the film's cinematic appeal and provided a visually captivating experience for moviegoers.

Chapter 7: Marketing and Promotion

The advertising of a film like "Bad Boys: Ride or Die" entails a multifaceted approach aimed at reaching a large audience, generating discussion, and building anticipation before its release. To engage and excite potential audiences, the film's promotional techniques included traditional marketing channels, digital platforms, strategic collaborations, and interactive experiences.

Traditional marketing outlets such as television, print media, and outdoor advertising were utilized to promote "Bad Boys: Ride or Die". This included running previews, TV advertisements, and promotional videos on major networks and cable channels to reach a large number of moviegoers. Print ads in magazines, newspapers, and entertainment media increased the film's visibility and recognition by targeting specific demographics and interests.

In addition to traditional media, digital marketing was crucial in promoting "Bad Boys: Ride or Die." The film's official website provided a one-stop shop for information, trailers, cast interviews, behind-the-scenes footage, and interactive features that captivated viewers and encouraged social media sharing. Social media platforms such as Facebook, Twitter, Instagram, and YouTube were used to share exclusive content, run contests, and interact with followers in real time, generating excitement and online buzz.

Strategic alliances and collaborations were another important promotional approach for the picture. This featured cross-promotions with other entertainment properties, businesses, and influencers in order to broaden reach and appeal to a diverse audience. Collaborations with music artists for soundtrack releases, tie-in items with popular businesses, and promotional events at big entertainment venues all contributed to synergy and leveraging existing fan bases to drive interest in "Bad Boys: Ride or Die."

Interactive interactions and immersive marketing efforts were used to engage consumers and create memorable experiences related to the film. This includes virtual reality (VR) experiences, augmented reality (AR) filters and games, interactive websites, and experiential events where fans could immerse themselves in the world of "Bad Boys: Ride or Die" and engage with film characters, sets, and props. These interactive components created a sense of excitement and immersion among fans, encouraging social sharing and word-of-mouth promotion.

Early screenings, press junkets, and promotional tours with the actors and filmmakers were scheduled to generate media attention, interviews, and reviews in the run-up to the film's release. This entailed utilizing media partnerships, attending industry events and conventions, and doing targeted outreach to key influencers, critics, and journalists to generate favorable buzz and anticipation for "Bad Boys: Ride or Die."

Innovative digital methods such as targeted web ads, influencer alliances, and data-driven marketing campaigns were used to reach specific audience segments and increase ticket sales. This comprised geo-targeted ads, personalized content recommendations, and social media influencers sharing sponsored material with their followers, which increased reach and engagement among relevant demographics.

The promotion of "Bad Boys: Ride or Die" took a comprehensive and integrated approach, leveraging traditional marketing channels, digital platforms, strategic partnerships, and interactive experiences to raise awareness, engage audiences, and drive excitement ahead of the film's release. Using a variety of methods and tactics, the promotional campaign effectively generated buzz, anticipation, and favorable word-of-mouth, contributing to the film's overall success and influence at the box office.

Trailer release and fan engagement

Trailer releases and fan participation were critical in advertising "Bad Boys: Ride or Die" and building anticipation among audiences ahead of its release. The deliberate release of trailers, teasers, and promotional films, together with interactive fan involvement initiatives, helped to build excitement and buzz for the picture.

The trailers for "Bad Boys: Ride or Die" were intentionally timed to promote excitement and buzz around the film. The initial teaser trailer gave viewers a glance into the film's world, promising action-packed sequences, character relationships, and crucial plot points. This teaser worked as a teaser campaign, building interest and laying the groundwork for future trailer releases.

Following the teaser, full-length trailers were produced to display additional footage, emphasize major characters, and provide more insight into the story, concepts, and visual spectacle of "Bad Boys: Ride or Die." To enhance reach and engagement, these trailers were selectively distributed across many platforms, including internet streaming platforms, social media outlets, and cinema previews.

Each trailer release was backed by a concerted marketing effort that includes internet promotions, social media advertising, and interactive fan experiences. Fans were invited to use designated hashtags to share and debate the trailers on social media channels, take part in trailer reaction videos and discussions, and interact with exclusive content released alongside the trailers.

Fan involvement initiatives were crucial to the promotional plan for "Bad Boys: Ride or Die." Fans were able to immerse themselves in the film's environment and engage with characters, scenes, and artifacts thanks to interactive experiences like virtual reality (VR), augmented reality (AR) filters, and interactive websites. These events not only sparked enthusiasm, but also motivated people to share their stories and promote the picture organically.

Fan contests, prizes, and giveaways were also established to reward fan loyalty and increase participation. Fans who actively participated in promotional activities, shared content, and exhibited their enthusiasm for "Bad Boys: Ride or Die" were eligible to win prizes such as special merchandise, advance screening tickets, and meet-and-greet chances with the cast.

Social media was important in fan engagement initiatives, with the film's official social media channels acting as hubs for updates, behind-the-scenes video, fan art exhibits, and interactive challenges. Fans were encouraged to submit fan art, make fan edits, and take part in film-themed challenges, developing a sense of community and camaraderie among them.

Live events and promotional tours with cast members and filmmakers increased fan engagement by allowing fans to meet with their favorite actors, attend special events, and participate in interactive activities related to the movie. These events sparked media attention, social media buzz, and word-of-mouth promotion, increasing fan enthusiasm and anticipation for "Bad Boys: Ride or Die."

Overall, the combination of strategic trailer releases, interactive fan engagement initiatives, and social media campaigns helped to build a loyal fan base, generate organic buzz, and create positive pre-release hype for "Bad Boys: Ride or Die," resulting in increased audience interest and box office success.

Conclusion

The production of "Bad Boys: Ride or Die" was a dynamic and collaborative process including a skilled team of filmmakers, actors, crew members, and creative experts working together to bring the film's vision to reality. Reflecting on the production of "Bad Boys: Ride or Die" reveals details about the creative process, problems encountered, and collaborative effort that contributed to the film's success.

The partnership between director Adil & Bilall, screenwriter Chris Bremner, and the cast and crew was an important part of the production of "Bad Boys: Ride or Die". The directing duo contributed their distinct vision and style to the film, infusing it with a mix of high-octane action, humorous moments, and character-driven storytelling. Chris Bremner's script laid a solid foundation, blending exhilarating sequences with intriguing character arcs and clever language to capture the heart of the "Bad Boys" franchise.

The cast of "Bad Boys: Ride or Die" was instrumental in bringing the characters to life and deepening the story. Will Smith and Martin Lawrence reprised their classic roles as Detectives Mike Lowrey and Marcus Burnett, bringing chemistry, humor, and charisma to the big screen. The film's ensemble cast, including Vanessa Hudgens, Alexander Ludwig, Paola Núñez, Eric Dane, Ioan Gruffudd, Jacob Scipio, Melanie Liburd, Tasha Smith, Tiffany Haddish, Joe Pantoliano, and DJ Khaled, delivered notable performances that enhanced the ensemble dynamic.

The production of "Bad Boys: Ride or Die" included extensive location shooting in Atlanta, Georgia and Miami, Florida, to depict the bright landscapes and dynamic environs that are central to the "Bad Boys" universe. The production design, costume design, and cinematography teams collaborated to create a visually appealing and immersive setting that represented the film's high-energy tone and urban feel.

One of the difficulties encountered during the filming of "Bad Boys: Ride or Die" was the impact of external variables such as the COVID-19 epidemic, which required changes to production schedules, safety measures, and logistical preparation. Despite these hurdles, the cast and crew's perseverance and dedication kept the film on track and true to its artistic vision.

The post-production phase of "Bad Boys: Ride or Die" included considerable editing, visual effects work, sound design, and score to fine-tune the film and bring all of its parts together smoothly. The teamwork of the editing team, visual effects artists, sound designers, composer Lorne Balfe, and the filmmaking team was critical in crafting the final cinematic experience.

Looking back on the production of "Bad Boys: Ride or Die," it is clear that the film's success was due to a collaborative effort, creative passion, and commitment to providing a thrilling and enjoyable cinematic experience. The collaborative attitude, new techniques, and dedication to storytelling brilliance all helped to make "Bad Boys: Ride or Die" a notable edition in the popular franchise.

www.ingramcontent.com/pod-product-compliance
Lightning Source LLC
Chambersburg PA
CBHW070402230526
45471CB00006B/2667